A GUIDED
gratitude
JOURNAL

DONNA WYLAND

COPYRIGHT NOTICE

A Guided Gratitude Journal

Scripture quotations taken from The Holy Bible, New International Version®, NIV®. Copyright © 1973, 1978, 1984, 2011 by Biblica, Inc. Used with permission of Zondervan. All rights reserved worldwide. www.zondervan.com

Cover and Interior Design: Lauren Skinner; Derinda Babcock
PUBLISHED BY: Donna Wyland, 5789 Kingston Place, Ave Maria, FL, 34142, 2025

_____

Library Cataloging Data
Names: Wyland, Donna (Donna Wyland)
Guided Gratitude Journal / Donna Wyland
198 p. 21.6 cm × 14 cm (8.5 in × 5.5 in.)
ISBN-13: 978-1-7328705-7-4 (paperback) | 978-1-7328705-8-1 (trade paperback) | 978-1-7328705-9-8 (ebook)

Key Words: motivational journal; gratitude journal for women; gratitude journal for men; thankful journal for women; grateful journal with prompts; grateful journal for women; inspirational journal

Library of Congress Control Number: 2025914819 Nonfiction

DEDICATION

To God, the Giver of all good things.
I am most grateful for You.

INTRODUCTION

If you look in a Merriam-Webster dictionary, you will see that the definition of gratitude is simply "the state of being grateful: Thankfulness." Not exactly compelling, to say the least, particularly when "being grateful" has the power to heal, energize, and improve relationships, spirituality, and overall mental and emotional health. Gratitude is a powerful state of being! How did Merriam-Webster miss that?

I much prefer the definition provided by Robert Emmons, PhD, Professor of Psychology at the University of California—Davis, and the world's leading scientific expert on gratitude: "Gratitude is an emotion of happiness and thankfulness for the good things in life." Though I still feel like they leave us wanting more, I like the fact they cite gratitude as an emotion and connect happiness and thankfulness to it. The truth is, it has been proven that cultivating a grateful attitude and centering our thoughts on thanksgiving, even for small blessings, can lead to a joyful state of being that attracts more blessing, which leads to greater gratitude, which leads to even more blessing. You get where I'm going with that.

Over the course of the past year, I have been conducting an informal study in my own life, paying greater attention to the thoughts in my mind which affect the emotions of my heart and, ultimately, my words and actions. In the end, that affects how I treat others and how they treat me in return. It is a profound rhythm of being, not unlike a roundabout where you have a choice to take one of four exits or continue circling around like Chevy Chase in *European Vacation*. How many times did he say, "There's Big Ben!" as he drove 'round and 'round without going anywhere?

This personal exercise of mine has yielded surprising and sometimes difficult statistics. For instance, I discovered that when I am disappointed by a situation or what someone I love says, I can ruminate for days on end, having complete conversations with them in my mind, though they are not present. I can't even imagine how many hours that has cost me over the many decades of my life. Yet *now* is God's time for me to wake up and change my thoughts, no longer being caught in the negative or the disappointing, but instead, focusing on a different, more positive situation or attitude to lift me above the negativity and its incredibly powerful pull.

This new way of processing and searching for the blessing has brought me hours of joy and led me to intimately understand the value of cultivating gratitude in my own life and helping others do the same. Now, if my husband forgets to pick up the drycleaning or decides to watch a "manly movie" in his den instead of replacing the filter or spraying for ants (which is very important in south Florida); I take a deep breath and thank God for giving my husband time to rest and giving me time to write or watch a Hallmark movie while I crochet or needlepoint a gift for someone I love. I can trust that important things will eventually be done.

I do not worry about people doing things in my timeframe anymore – or at least not nearly as much as I used to. I trust that what needs to be done will get done, and if something goes wrong, it is not my fault, nor do I need to fix it. I can let others be in charge of their own lives and focus on the life God is leading me to live. What a relief!

We don't need to manage everyone and everything. It is important to allow others to follow their own journey as God leads them and they respond according to His timing, not our own. It rarely happens fast enough for us, but that's not in our power, nor is it our responsibility.

I pray that this guided journal brings you relief and peace and leads you to the wonderful state of mind where gratitude reigns and the rest falls away. Gratitude is God's gift. His way of keeping us in the middle of the "peace that passes all understanding" and blessing us with unmitigated joy that surprises, delights, and lifts us above everyday worries, anxieties, and fears.

We have multiple choices to make all day, every day. Will we choose to see the beauty and gifts of God, or will we get lost in the spiral of negativity that leads to depression, illness, sadness, and shame?

I believe we all have the ability to choose gratitude. Choose joy. Choose to be courageous enough to believe that God is always at work and good things *do* come to those who love Him. If my personal experience this past year has taught me anything, it has taught me that God has wonderful plans for all of us. If we pray for eyes to see and ears to hear, He will answer and show us every reason we have to be grateful each day.

May you be blessed as you search for His gifts in your life and may this Guided Gratitude Journal become a legacy of your journey to joy, emotional and physical health, peace, and a thankful way of life. Make it an annual commitment to record everything God is doing in and through you. I promise you, He is always up to something very good.

He sees you. He loves you. He is excited to hear your praises and watch you grow into a gratitude-filled man or woman of God who lights the world on fire simply by being your wonderful, beautiful, joyful self.

"I cannot tell you anything that, in a few minutes, will tell you how to be rich. But I can tell you how to feel rich, which is far better, let me tell you firsthand, than being rich.

BE GRATEFUL...

It's the only totally reliable get-rich-quick scheme."

—BEN STEIN, Actor, comedian, economist

"Gratitude is the healthiest of all human emotions. The more you express gratitude for what you have, the more likely you will have even more to express gratitude for."
—Zig Ziglar

We have all heard the adage "Cleanliness is next to godliness," but I believe *gratitude* should have the seat of honor at the godliness table. Living in a state of gratitude lifts us higher spiritually, mentally, and emotionally until we can feel the light of God filling us, surrounding us wherever we go. Gratitude is considered the healthiest of all human emotions because it has the power to heal what hurts, restore what was broken, and inspire us to create a beautiful life.

List three things (people, nature, hobbies, circumstances, rest...) you are most grateful for:

_____

_____

_____

_____

What would your world be like without them in your life?

_____

_____

_____

_____

_____

How and when will you express gratitude for each of them today/this week?

_____

_____

_____

_____

_____

What positive thoughts and feelings did you experience as a result of this exercise?

_____

_____

_____

_____

_____

Begin today to use the journal pages at the back of this book to list at least three things or people you are grateful for each day. Be consistent and be specific. Why are you grateful for each person, thing, or situations?

**"Reflect upon your present blessings, of
which every man has plenty;
not on your past misfortunes,
of which all men have some."
—Charles Dickens**

Why is it so much easier to think of the many things that have gone wrong or bad decisions we made versus thinking about the numerous things that were, and still are, positive and life-giving? I must have more than twenty journals tucked into several boxes in which I recorded my thoughts, feelings, prayers, and blessings. I can assure you that I wrote a lot more about the struggles and trials than I did about the good things and answered prayers.

Thankfully, God is changing that and speaking to me about the power of words and thoughts, spoken and unspoken, that can defer a destiny or light a soul on fire. I, for one, want to be the light on a hill that brings peace and joy and draws others closer to God. I am guessing you want that too.

Name two circumstances in the past that did not go as you hoped they would. What happened?

_____

_____

_____

_____

Describe any blessings you now recognize occurred because of those experiences.

_____

_____

_____

_____

_____

_____

What positive changes have you made as a result of experiencing those situations?

_____

_____

_____

_____

_____

_____

_____

**"Give thanks in all circumstances;
for this is the will of God in Christ Jesus
for you."
—1 Thes. 5:18**

Giving thanks in all circumstances is not an easy task. When we lose people we love or endure abuse from someone we thought we could trust, the furthest thing from our minds is giving thanks. We are grieving. Surviving. Struggling to get by and get through. Yet this is the will of God in Christ Jesus for us. To give thanks in all circumstances.

Sometimes we don't see the blessing until we get to the other side and recognize the strength and courage we gained and the beautiful way God protected us in the midst of the storm. Perhaps we won't have the desire to praise God for a particular situation until we stand with Him in heaven.

Either way, it's the attitude of our heart that connects us to the Father and draws Him closer to hold us and comfort us through the hard times. And when His blessings are showered upon us in a season of favor and we praise Him with unceasing gratitude, we remember that He is always good and always near. His abundant blessings never run out.

Describe where you are today. Is this an easy day to give thanks or one that requires great faith?

_____

_____

_____

_____

_____

_____

_____

_____

_____

_____

What are you praying God will accomplish in or through you this week or year?

_____

_____

_____

_____

_____

_____

_____

_____

_____

_____

_____

_____

How does it feel to give thanks to God in the midst of your current circumstances? Do you feel His presence and pleasure as you surrender and choose to be grateful despite confusion or uncertainty?

_____

_____

_____

_____

_____

_____

_____

_____

_____

_____

_____

_____

_____

"There is a calmness to a life lived in gratitude. A quiet joy."
—Ralph H. Blum

I spent thirty years competing in business, modeling, publishing, and even parenting. Maybe you can relate. When our children don't live up to our expectations, we can take it personally and feel like we've failed. When I was a model, I was so concerned about *not* being overweight that I lost TOO much weight and was told to gain it back. In business and publishing there is always someone brighter, smarter, more famous, or more successful. These types of competition never lead us where we truly long to be.

Competition does not lead to confidence. Pretending to be more than we are does not lead to peace. And faking it never leads to freedom. God's design for us has always been authenticity, wholeness, and connection. We are to encourage one another, not feel envy or resentment. Gratitude for what we *do* have is a critical component of our journey toward abundance, prosperity, unity, and peace. Isn't that what we all really want?

On a scale of 1 to 10, how would you rate your current level of gratitude and peace? What is the reason for your rating?

_____

_____

_____

_____

_____

_____

_____

_____

_____

_____

When have you experienced the joy of being authentic and connecting with others based on who you truly are? Beyond being joyful, how did you feel?

_____

_____

_____

_____

_____

_____

_____

_____

_____

_____

_____

_____

If you struggle with comparison, what is one step you can take today to bring yourself into alignment with God's design for authenticity, wholeness, and connection? Write your action step as a prayer to God as you wait with expectancy for His answer.

_____

_____

_____

_____

_____

_____

_____

_____

_____

_____

_____

_____

Author Brene Brown wrote, "Few things are more uncomfortable than being vulnerable, but standing outside the arena, missing moments of life, can be even more uncomfortable." Consider reading her excellent book titled *Daring Greatly* to learn how to create a powerful vision and open the door to allow yourself to be seen.

**"Enter his gates with thanksgiving and
his courts with praise; give thanks to
him and praise his name."
—Psalm 100:4**

Biblical scholars teach that the prayers of God's people, offered from hearts filled with thanksgiving, open His heavenly gates to those who call upon Him in faith. Many scripture verses reveal how God protects, defends, blesses, and leads His people in response to prayer. In a typical day, how often do we remember to give thanks to the LORD and praise His name opening those heavenly gates and God's heart?

Morning times of Bible reading and prayer often yield moments of praise, but imagine the joy of our LORD upon hearing us day and night, without ceasing, calling out to Him, seeking wisdom, healing, and direction with thankful hearts. How it must touch *His* heart to be blessed by our praise. And when we praise with grateful hearts, the angels in heaven rejoice and we are filled with peace.

How often do you sit or walk with the LORD and express thanksgiving through praise? Write a short prayer describing your thanksgiving for this day.

_____

_____

_____

_____

_____

_____

_____

_____

_____

Take a moment to think about the enormity of God opening the gates of heaven to you when you praise His name. What do you imagine He feels as He is opening the gates and His heart to you?

_____

_____

_____

_____

_____

_____

_____

What area of life is God calling you to trust Him with as you praise and thank Him for what He is doing and what you can trust He will continue to do? What are you expectantly waiting for Him to do or intervene in to change?

_____

_____

_____

_____

_____

_____

_____

_____

_____

_____

_____

_____

_____

_____

_____

_____

_____

_____

"Learn to be thankful for what you already have while you pursue all that you want."
—Jim Rohn

I hate to admit it but this idea of being thankful for what I have was lost on me until I was in my 50s. Until that time, there were always mountains to climb and accomplishments to achieve. I literally had a license plate that said GOALSTR (Goal Setter). Then, when I became a Certified Christian Life Coach, I heard about the marvelous idea of celebrating your successes before moving on to a new goal. What a great idea! Who doesn't like an opportunity to pat themselves on the back and appreciate what they've accomplished? Or take a moment to thank God and others who helped you succeed?

I think we should all embrace this idea and teach it to our children as well. When we earn something, overcome an obstacle, or even learn a new skill, we should all take a moment to thank God for what we've accomplished before we plunge headfirst into our next pursuit. Breathe. Celebrate. Recalibrate. Go!

That is the rhythm of the goal setter who knows how to balance each accomplishment with a celebration, even if it's a party of one.

Name three to five things you are thankful for today:

_____

_____

_____

_____

_____

_____

_____

_____

_____

Describe the most recent time you celebrated the achievement of a goal. How did it make you feel? In what way did it encourage you to pursue your next goal or dream?

_____

_____

_____

_____

_____

_____

_____

_____

_____

_____

_____

_____

_____

_____

_____

_____

_____

What is one goal you are currently working toward? How will you celebrate your accomplishment of that goal? Who will you include in your celebration?

_____

_____

_____

_____

_____

_____

_____

> **"Do not be anxious about anything, but in every situation, by prayer and petition, with thanksgiving, present your requests to God."**
> **—Phil. 4:6**

Not be anxious about anything? That's a tall order for anyone, even those of us who believe in God and trust that He loves us and will bring good out of every situation. Yet we can learn how to trust God more by praying and petitioning Him knowing He hears and cares.

When my daughter was a teen, she was demonstrating visible signs of depression and anxiety. I felt powerless to help as I watched her fall deeper and deeper into isolation and pain. Then one day, God prompted me and my daughter at the same time to consider boarding school to remove her from the people and situations that were causing her pain and give her time to heal.

I hated the idea of her being away from home and away from me, but I hated even more what she was going through. Over the following three months, we researched, visited boarding schools, and prayed for clear guidance from God. He took her to a boarding school where another new student—a girl my daughter's age—was also a Christian. They became fast friends and were used by God to comfort fellow teammates when one of the girls on the volleyball team was killed in a tragic auto accident.

God led my daughter away from me, but He led her to a perfect place for her to begin to breathe and heal and restore her joy. Through it all, I lifted my daughter in prayer and surrendered to God my own plans for her. He had an open door to do marvelous things in and through her. I praise Him today for His great love and presence in her life as she continues to allow Him to transform her in ways that amaze me and bless her and my own mother-heart.

What situation in your life is causing you anxiety and stress?

_____

_____

_____

_____

_____

_____

_____

_____

_____

_____

What is holding you back from trusting God with it? Do you truly believe He hears your prayers and petitions and that He will answer you in the best way in His time?

_____

_____

_____

_____

_____

_____

_____

_____

Write a prayer to God thanking Him for all He has done in your life and asking Him to help you trust Him more. Include a prayer for courage to surrender your decisions and anxieties to Him. Then continue to pray in confident hope and praise each day as you anticipate His answer.

_____

_____

_____

_____

_____

_____

> "I would maintain that thanks are the highest form of thought, and that gratitude is happiness doubled by wonder."
> —Gilbert K. Chesterton

I have been learning a lot the past two years about the power of maintaining a positive attitude and focusing on things that make my soul sing. The difference I have noticed in my overall level of joy is astonishing. I believe gratitude has been the foundational reason for that change.

Until recently, I think I let the challenges of life take up residence in my mind, causing my attitude to swing between forced happiness, fake happiness, and overwhelm. I spent so much time focusing on what was wrong in my life that I had little to no capacity to discover solutions to the challenges I faced.

Now I wake up each morning with an attitude that, no matter what happens, God will give me the wisdom and strength to face and overcome it. I have more energy and attract more positive people who want to help me succeed. Doors are opening that I believe would not have been opened if I still lived with a mind overwhelmed by the trials of life. They are still very much present, but I choose to focus on finding solutions and taking action.

Are you drowning in debt? The old adage 'spend less and earn more' is still true today. Find a way to reduce expenses and earn a little extra cash. Trust God to surprise you in ways you never expected as He did for me when I was walking through a devastating divorce. Struggling in a relationship? Pray about what the root cause of the issue is. Sometimes God allows us to put distance between ourselves and another person to give us both time to cool down and seek a new perspective on the situation. Sometimes, we just need to let go and pray they find their own joy as they travel along their personal life path. You don't have to be pulled down by them. Try to lift them up, then let go and give the relationship to God.

Gratitude is absolutely the shining star on top of happiness that changes everything. Practice it every day and you will find your life being transformed in wonderful ways.

What three things are you most grateful for today?

_____

_____

_____

_____

_____

_____

_____

_____

_____

_____

If you could change one thing in your life, what would it be?

_____

_____

_____

_____

_____

_____

_____

_____

_____

Express gratitude to God for trusting you with that situation or person. Describe one step you will take to begin to rectify the situation or move toward resolution or relief. When will you take that step and who will help hold you accountable to your plan?

_____

_____

_____

_____

"Give thanks to the LORD, for he is good.
His love endures forever."
—Psalm 136:1

When life is going well and we feel connected and loved, it is easier to thank the LORD and believe that He is good. But what about those times when we're walking through frustration, illness, anger, or pain? How do we connect with God and thank Him for that? How do we trust that He is still good and His love for us has not changed?

I have had a lot of experience with the struggles of life, sometimes due to my own decisions and choices, and sometimes the cause of other people's actions and words. It would have been so easy to give up on God and try to figure things out on my own, but I believe God held on so tight that that was not an option for me.

You see, when the deepest pain came and the greatest tragedies struck, I was already so used to sitting with God, Bible open on my lap, coffee mug on the table beside me, that it was habit, a routine that was so much a part of my life that it felt uncomfortable to change. I thank and praise God for that because those were the days when He spoke directly to my soul and showered me with love and filled my heart with hope.

I never gave up on Him because He was already so ingrained in my daily life that I did not want to give up. I wanted to hold onto hope that He would intervene, and I would be okay. And that is exactly what happened. I had to endure some very difficult years to get to a place of freedom, peace, and joy, but God held my hand and loved me and walked with me through each day, increasing my faith and my strength. There is no doubt in my mind that God *is* good, and His love truly does endure forever through all circumstances.

What are your current thoughts about God and His love and goodness? How do you connect with Him each day to open your heart to receive all He has to offer you?

_____

_____

_____

_____

_____

_____

_____

_____

_____

_____

_____

_____

_____

_____

_____

_____

_____

_____

Describe a current circumstance that is causing you frustration, anger, or pain. What do you want God to do? How do you want Him to intervene to relieve the pressure and bring His love and goodness to the situation? Are you willing to surrender the situation to Him and trust Him with the outcome?

_____

_____

_____

_____

_____

_____

_____

Write a prayer of gratitude to God for the work He will do in that circumstance. Being by writing, "I thank and praise you, Father God, that I can trust You to..." Ask Holy Spirit to fill your heart with hope and peace. And at the end, surrender the circumstance, person, and your preferred outcome to Him, trusting He has a wonderful plan to bring good from it.

_____

_____

_____

_____

_____

_____

_____

_____

_____

_____

_____

_____

_____

_____

_____

_____

_____

_____

"Gratitude is when memory is stored in the heart and not in the mind."
—Lionel Hampton

When I think of my mom, I think of how grateful I am for her love and support, and for the many ways she displayed kindness to those around her. She was the woman who talked to the boy bagging her groceries, got to know the family of the receptionist at the doctor's office, and volunteered to cook meals for anyone going through a difficult time.

She longed to be an elementary school teacher like her mother, but when she and my dad had four children in the span of six years, her plans were relegated to the corner of her life. She tried to take night classes when dad was home, but the four of us were too much for him to handle.

Despite giving up her dream, she lived a life of gratitude talking about what she was thankful for with little thought for what she had hoped would be. She stored in her heart and treasured the things and people who meant the most to her and chose not to focus on the losses and disappointments that surely lived in her head. She clung to memories that made her feel grateful instead and blessed all of us around her with her positive attitude.

What memories are you storing in your heart? Are they primarily memories that lead to gratitude or do you struggle to find things to be grateful for?

_____

_____

_____

_____

_____

_____

_____

_____

_____

Describe someone in your life who you believe stores memories of gratitude in their heart. How do they express their gratitude: through words, actions, prayers, or something else?

_____

_____

_____

_____

_____

_____

_____

_____

_____

_____

_____

_____

_____

_____

_____

_____

_____

_____

_____

What is the first thought that flows regularly through your mind that you will bathe in thoughts and prayers of gratitude? If it is a difficult thought or emotion that causes you to feel pain, regret, or negativity, name one small way God brought something good from the situation. Consider forgiving someone else or forgiving yourself so you can be free.

_____

_____

_____

_____

"Save us, LORD our God, and gather us from the nations, that we may give thanks to your holy name and glory in your praise."
—Psalm 106:47

This verse would not mean as much to us today if we had not survived the COVID pandemic, senseless wars, and the cultural struggles of our time as we fight to keep God's values and precepts in the center of our lives. God has absolutely saved us from many devastating things and gathered our families closer as we pray for restoration, freedom, and peace.

Without God, there is no hope. He is worthy of our thanksgiving (gratitude) and praise.

As a survivor of psychological, spiritual, and emotional abuse, I have an intimate knowledge of God's presence and goodness. He held my hand as I walked though eighteen years of that abuse, and He strengthened me inside, gave me a voice, and helped me walk away when the time was right. He is always near, even when we can't feel Him there.

Years ago, when I attended a women's conference, Jill Briscoe told a story about a friend of hers who was struggling with breast cancer. Her friend said, "Jill, I can't feel God's presence," to which Jill replied, "When you can't feel Him with your heart, feel Him with your *faith*."

I never forgot that powerful story. Throughout my years of abuse, I clung to the truth that I could feel God with my faith when I was unable to feel Him with my heart because my heart was so bruised and beaten down. I invite you to do the same so that your life will reflect His glory and grace and your heart will be filled with gratitude for His presence and love.

When or where do you normally feel God's presence in your life? Can you feel Him with your heart, or are you in a season of needing to feel Him with your faith?

_____

_____

_____

_____

_____

_____

_____

_____

_____

_____

Are you able to praise God in the trials and pain? If so, how is your life impacted through your praise? Is your heart filled with peace? Do you feel more joy?

Are you inspired to connect more? To share thoughts and feelings with others?

_____

_____

_____

_____

_____

_____

_____

_____

_____

What difficult journey are you facing today? Reaffirm your faith in God and write a prayer of praise to express how grateful you are for His presence and promise to protect, comfort, and provide whatever you need to get through to the other side.

_____

_____

_____

_____

_____

_____

_____

"When Gratitude becomes an essential foundation in our lives, miracles start to appear everywhere."
—Unknown

Have you ever experienced a time when circumstances seem to just fall into place and all sorts of good things begin to happen at the same time? Doors begin to open without you asking. Positive movement begins to take place in an area where you were stuck for months, or even years. Have you ever wondered why that is? What state of mind were you in? Was God feeling your gratitude and praise and showering you with favor as a result?

I am currently walking through such a season. After struggling for nearly twenty years to push doors open and capture a publisher's attention, God sent Deb Haggerty at Elk Lake Publishing, Inc. to encourage me and publish my books. Seven years later (a very biblical number that means "completion, healing, promises fulfilled"), doors are opening to teach and coach and start a local writer's group, and I am being greatly blessed. The thing is, I didn't look for clients to coach or ask to be an instructor at a writer's conference. I didn't even inquire as to how to start a local writer's group. Yet, God is placing these opportunities in my path at an age when many women are retiring. While they are enjoying family, golf, or travel, I am being asked to trust God to fill me with energy to work, mentor, and teach.

I am a bit nervous because I am not yet fully equipped to do all of those things, yet I trust that God will carry me through to my "mini miracles." I am filled with gratitude and am willing to try. There is so much connection between gratitude and miracles whether healing miracles or the tiny, everyday kind of miracles that God may use in a much bigger way. For everything there is a season, and the season for gratitude and miracles brings a year-round kind of blessing.

What is God surprising you with today? What "mini miracle"—or tremendously large miracle—is God working in and around your life and the lives of those you love?

_____

_____

_____

_____

_____

_____

_____

_____

_____

_____

_____

_____

_____

_____

_____

_____

What are you most grateful for today? What doors is God opening for you? What doors is your heart yearning for Him to open?

_____

_____

_____

_____

_____

_____

_____

_____

_____

_____

_____

_____

_____

_____

_____

Who do you share your gratitude with? Who in your life knows about the open doors and miracles God has shown you and worked in and though you? How has this sharing encouraged your faith and the faith of the person you shared with?

_____

_____

_____

_____

_____

_____

_____

_____

_____

_____

_____

**"So then, just as you received Christ
Jesus as Lord, continue to live your
lives in him, rooted and built up in
him, strengthened in the faith as you
were taught, and overflowing with
thankfulness."**
—Col. 2:7

As stated in Luke 6:45, "out of the overflow of our
hearts, the mouth speaks," and boy, have I noticed
the connection over the years. When we overflow
with thankfulness in our hearts and minds, our
faith is strengthened and the people around us are
encouraged by the words we speak.

When I married my current husband after many
years of abuse, I learned that, as a result of that
abuse, I had developed a communication style
that was disrespectful. My mind was still filled
with negative thoughts which affected my heart,
words and actions, which negatively impacted our
marriage. Thankfully, God led me to books and
podcasts and His Word to teach me how to speak
and react with love, grace, and respect.

My faith was built over those abusive years but so was an enormous brick wall around my heart. I vowed that I would never again be hurt and controlled by another human being, but I hadn't learned how to let the right people in, how to live my life in Christ as a lover of Him and others. I am so grateful God used many leaders, authors, and friends to teach me how to communicate in love, and I am grateful my husband and I can walk together down this road of faith, learning day by day how to live in truth and peace.

Name three things you are overflowing with thankfulness for today. They can be as simple as being thankful for the sunshine, for the birds that sing in your backyard, for flowers that bloom, or for a healthy breakfast to strengthen your body for the day ahead.

_____

_____

_____

_____

_____

_____

_____

_____

_____

_____

Who is helping you to "live your life in Christ, rooted and built up in Him, and strengthened in faith"? How will you express your gratitude to them for their gift of encouragement and time? If you don't have someone special helping you in this way, pray for God to show you someone who might become that person. Make a short list of people you believe could be that for you and lay it before God as you pray.

_____

_____

_____

_____

_____

_____

_____

_____

_____

_____

_____

_____

_____

_____

_____

_____

If you have ever made the mistake of expressing yourself in a disrespectful way, what did you do to correct the situation? Did you seek forgiveness or receive counseling to learn how to speak and act with grace, respect, and love? Have you ever said these powerful words: "I love you. I am sorry. Please forgive me for (be specific)"? If you need to say that to someone today, I pray that God will give you the courage to do so to restore wholeness and joy to your relationship and life. Use these lines to write what you will say to that person. When will you ask for their forgiveness?

_____

_____

_____

_____

_____

_____

_____

_____

_____

_____

_____

_____

_____

"Gratitude turns what we have
into enough."
—Anonymous

Would you walk away from a millionaire's lifestyle if it meant you would be free of abuse, control, and physical illness that resulted from the stress of being in that relationship? Most people would have to ponder that question for quite a while. God gave me an opportunity to live that Top 1% lifestyle to teach me in a powerful way that money can be used for good or to control and dominate others.

It took me two attempts to make the final break. Thinking of what I was giving up after eighteen years of living that lifestyle was difficult. Would I spend the rest of my life alone? How was I going to support myself after being out of the corporate world for so long? Which friends would stay with him and which would show love to me by supporting me? It was one of the most difficult times of my life, but ultimately God showed me a better way.

My current husband and I both said we knew the day we met that there was something special between us. A dear friend had encouraged me to make a Wish List of sorts detailing the attributes I needed, wanted, and would like to have (Bonus!) in a man. So, I made a list alright. It ended up being two pages long on both sides. I left no stone unturned. And when I met my current husband, every single one of those boxes got checked EXCEPT for one. Financially Independent.

That's a biggie for us women who have a great need for stability and security. I had hoped to find an entrepreneur who owned his own business and had the funds and flexibility to travel and enjoy life with me between work commitments. That was the lifestyle I was used to, and I prayed God would bring it to me again. My new guy, however, had a regular job that required him to show up Monday through Friday, from 8:00 a.m. to 4:30 p.m. with three weeks of vacation. I was not thrilled. Yet he had every other attribute I was seeking.

I prayed hard, questioned what I was doing even as I was dating him and falling in love. Then, after saying yes when he proposed, I prayed and sensed God saying, "Not yet." I gave the ring back and told him Holy Spirit said no. I have never seen a more confused expression on a man's face. Several months later, we began to date again, and now we are about to celebrate our 5th anniversary.

Are we millionaires? No. But I am grateful. Grateful for a man who truly loves the Lord and me. Grateful to be partnered with someone who listens and respects me as I respect him. Grateful for our children and grandchildren and the quirky way we are blending them all together. Grateful... And what we have is truly enough.

What do you wish you had? Do you pray for more money, a new love relationship, friendship, or health? What do you believe having those things would bring to your life?

_____

_____

_____

_____

_____

_____

_____

_____

What are you grateful for that is already present in your life? List all of the little things that help to make your life feel like it is "enough". Continue on a separate piece of paper if necessary.

_____

_____

_____

_____

_____

_____

_____

_____

_____

_____

_____

_____

_____

_____

_____

_____

_____

Review your list of what you are grateful for. Which things can you easily say are "enough"? Which things are you praying God will help you *feel* like they are "enough"? Which things would you like to improve or work toward accomplishing to reach the place of being "enough"? It's okay to want more. God created us and the desires of our hearts.

Being honest here is very important as it will show you where to focus your prayers, petitions, and praises to God and will begin to give you a roadmap to show you where you sense God wants you to go. You'll also see more clearly what you need to do to get you where you want to be.

**"I thank my God every time
I remember you."
—Phil. 1:3**

Who do you think of when you read that verse?
Who do you thank God for every time you remember
them? I laugh because there are many people in my
life who I thank God for *most* of the time, but *every*
time would be a stretch. As human beings, we have
a way of saying the wrong thing or frustrating others
or disappointing them without even trying. I am
pretty sure they would not be thanking God for me
at that time, nor would I be thanking God for them
if I were on the receiving end of someone's anger,
disappointment, or wrath.

The first people that come to mind are family
members. I am thankful for my husband, but,
oh how he can drive me crazy sometimes. Same
for our daughters and grandchildren. They are
completely lovable, and each has a good heart, but
sometimes they cross a line and make requests that
are inappropriate or just plain outlandish. Because

I have a hard time saying no but am working on it, I am not generally thanking God for those difficult conversations or for the person who made the request.

Still, no matter what happens in our relationships, whether at home, at church, in the community, or at work, God has given us hearts to quickly forgive and return to a loving place. I am constantly surprised by the speed at which God will convict me of thoughts or feelings that, although entirely justifiable, do not line up with His heart and will. Quick conviction brings speedy repentance, and suddenly the love comes pouring back into my heart and the grievance that seemed so large the previous day has shrunk to the size of a pea. Soon, it disappears and I am praising God again for that person, that circumstance, for the lesson I learned about myself in the midst of the challenge.

Who do you thank God for every time—or almost every time—you remember them? What is it about that person that fills your heart with gratitude when you think of them?

_____

_____

_____

_____

_____

_____

_____

Who do you have a harder time thanking God for? What causes you to feel that way?

_____

_____

_____

_____

_____

_____

_____

Describe a time someone you love caused you to feel less than grateful for them? What were you feeling and why? How was the situation resolved? Where is your relationship today?

_____

_____

_____

_____

_____

_____

_____

_____

_____

_____

_____

_____

_____

_____

_____

_____

_____

_____

_____

_____

_____

List 10 people that quickly come to mind who you are thankful to God for today. List 3 adjectives next to their names that describe the positive attributes you see in them or their lives.

_____

_____

_____

_____

_____

_____

_____

_____

_____

_____

_____

_____

_____

_____

_____

Now list 3 people that you struggle with on a regular basis and briefly describe why.

_____

_____

_____

_____

_____

_____

_____

_____

Vow to praise and thank God each day for the 10 people you are most grateful for and make a commitment to pray love and joy into the lives of the 3 people you struggle with. Allow this practice to become a daily habit and watch to see what God will do in their hearts and in yours as He transforms you through the power of His unconditional love.

**"Gratitude makes sense of our past,
brings peace for today, and creates a
vision for tomorrow."
—Melody Beattie**

How many of us spend too much time reliving the past, walking in anxiety about today, and at a complete loss about the future because we are worried about finances, health, children and grandchildren, the state of our country, the world, and so on? Life can fill us with dread or open our hearts and minds to the possibility of a bright future. Which side do you generally find yourself on?

Here's the truth. We cannot change the past. We can seek help to heal it, but we cannot change it. Today is a *present* from God. He allowed us to wake up, to have another shot at making a difference, creating something beautiful to share with the world. If we wallow in a bed of indecision and confusion, we can waste the precious days, months, and years we have without accomplishing much or feeling the freedom and joy God created us to live in. Gratitude can change all of that and give us a positive outlook for the future no matter what we face today.

Here is my vision for tomorrow:

- World peace, and no, it's not a pat beauty pageant answer (though I was Mrs. Ohio America and 3rd runner-up to Mrs. America in 1999). I truly believe world peace is possible.

- Churches that truly shine the love and light of Christ and welcome all to know and be loved by him.

- Free education. Again, I totally believe this is possible and is on God's heart to do.

- Freedom and prosperity for all so we can pursue what we are passionate about instead of punch a clock and struggle to make ends meet.

- Create, create, create! I love to make things with my hands and design new products like I did a long time ago when I had an inspirational gift shop. Creating beauty where there was none, being inspired by Holy Spirit to bring something beautiful into the world, lights my fire.

- More books. I love to write and have ideas for at least three more books.

- Love that conquers hate and brings a sense of security and safety to all.

- Travel, travel, travel! There are so many beautiful places I would love to visit. My husband isn't as much of a traveler as I am, but he is willing to go because it makes me happy.

- Families restored and connected and supportive of one another.

I could go on and on. These are the things that fill my mind and heart and prayers each day. I believe God has a wonderful future for all of us, and I'm sticking with it. Now it's your turn.

What are you most grateful for from your past? It could be a deceased relative who encouraged you, a teacher who saw in you what you couldn't see in yourself, an event, etc. Why are you grateful for the experience, the lesson learned, or the event?

_____

_____

_____

_____

_____

_____

_____

_____

_____

_____

_____

_____

What are you grateful for that brings peace instead of confusion, guilt, or frustration?

_____

_____

_____

_____

_____

_____

_____

_____

_____

_____

_____

What vision do you have for tomorrow? How do you see gratitude supporting your hope for the future? What do you believe by faith will come to pass to encourage your vision?

_____

_____

_____

_____

_____

**"Thanks be to God for his
indescribable gift!"
—2 Cor. 9:15**

As you read that verse, you may ask, What 'indescribable gift'? This section of 2 Corinthians is describing the beautiful cycle of reaping and sowing. Verse 11 states, "You will be made rich in every way so that you can be generous on every occasion, and through us your generosity will result in thanksgiving to God." There's that word again — thanksgiving... gratitude... to God.

Do these verses refer only to being generous with money? With service to those in need? Interestingly, Paul includes the following promise in verse 13, "... men will praise God for the obedience that accompanies your confession of the gospel of Christ..." So, step one is our confession of the gospel of Christ which, to me, means sharing our testimony, the powerful story of how God activated His Spirit within us to draw us to Him and transform our lives from the routine of everyday living to become like Him, full of joy, patience, peace, and love.

That is what causes people to praise God before they even get to the part of receiving help and money when they are in need. Basic needs are critical but so is providing for their spirits by sharing our stories, our testimonies of the love of God and His power to save and change us into meaningful, courageous people who serve Him.

The most important gift God gives to those in spiritual need is the gift of His love and forgiveness. All our sins are washed away, never to be remembered by God again. *That's* the indescribable gift! God's amazing grace.

I have recently been sensing God calling me to share my testimony. It won't be easy because I have a definite before-Jesus/after-Jesus life story, but it's a story He wants me to tell, and I pray many feel His overwhelming love and receive His grace as a result of hearing it.

What does your relationship with God/Jesus/Holy Spirit mean to you? When did your relationship with God begin? Who helped you connect with Him in a personal way?

_____

_____

_____

_____

_____

_____

_____

_____

_____

_____

Describe how you and your life have changed since knowing Jesus as Lord and Savior. If you have not yet accepted Christ as Lord and Savior and you'd like to make that decision, simply confess your sins to Him, ask Him to come into your heart to live and move and transform your life into the new creation the Bible promises you will be. Receive His love and forgiveness.

_____

_____

_____

_____

_____

_____

_____

_____

_____

Write about your thoughts and feelings regarding your decision to ask Jesus into your heart. Commit to Him your love and devotion and ask Him to fill you with wisdom and guide your decisions today and the rest of your life. If you prayed that prayer, welcome to the family of God! You are dearly loved, chosen, and free to be who God created you to be!

_____

_____

_____

_____

_____

_____

_____

_____

_____

_____

_____

_____

_____

_____

_____

_____

_____

List the highlights of your life story and the circumstances that led you to Christ. Is there a definite "before-Christ" and "after-Christ" element to your testimony? In what area do you believe He has changed you the most? If you just prayed to receive

Christ into your heart, what area of your life do you most want God to move in to change and transform the way you live?

_____

_____

_____

_____

_____

_____

_____

_____

_____

_____

_____

_____

If you feel God calling you to share your personal testimony, commit to answer that call today. If you just asked Jesus into your heart, tell a friend, family member, or someone at a church to share the wonderful news. I praise God in heaven for offering His indescribable gift to you and pray He uses you to bring healing, grace, and forgiveness to others too. You are loved. You are chosen. You are free.

> "Gratitude connects us to others
> and feeling gratitude allows us to be our
> best selves. When we are truly grateful,
> we can count on living the life
> we want."
>
> **—Anonymous**

While I work to be grateful each day for the many blessings I have, I am known to be a goal setter and dreamer, always looking to the future with excitement and expectancy. My mother often said, "Get your head out of the clouds," when I was in my teens. There was something about our small country town that did not fill my needs. My soul wanted so much more. My heart yearned for a bigger life, for experiences and adventures that I could not foresee happening near our tiny home off Route 229 between the cornfields and farms.

Today, I realize how very blessed I was to grow up in a small town near so many people who loved me and looked out for me. I missed the gratitude of being connected to others in a deeper way as I focused on the future to bring me my greatest, wished-for joy. Now I understand intimately the value of being my best self, of serving and caring for others without so much concern about myself, my goals, and dreams.

I finally know the secret. Being grateful for all things, accepting what *is*, is one of life's greatest gifts. That's not to say we shouldn't dream and work to make those dreams come true. The secret to living the life we want is by loving the life we *have*. Dream your dreams. Set your goals. But do not forget to be wide awake to the blessings of this day.

Would you consider yourself to be more of a realist or a dreamer? If you're a realist, I challenge you to dream. What would you do if you had no fear, no doubt, no financial worries? Be grateful that God is awakening that dream. If you are a dreamer, set both feet firmly on the ground and look around. What are you most grateful for this present day?

_____

_____

_____

_____

_____

_____

_____

_____

_____

Describe the life you want to live. Include everything related to family, friends, work, hobbies, finances, spiritual life, home, and more...

_____

_____

_____

_____

_____

_____

_____

_____

_____

_____

_____

_____

_____

_____

_____

_____

_____

_____

_____

_____

_____

_____

_____

_____

_____

What is one step you can take toward loving yourself and your life today while you look to the future and move toward the life you want to live?

_____

_____

_____

_____

_____

_____

_____

_____

_____

_____

_____

**"There are only two ways to live
your life. One is as though nothing
is a miracle. The other is as though
everything is a miracle."**
—Albert Einstein

Have you ever witnessed a miracle? Who's to
say we haven't all born witness to multiple miracles
in our lifetimes without realizing it? I have heard
of physical healings taking place and accidents
avoided by a miraculous hand of protection and
grace, but the first miracle that comes to mind for
me personally is that of answered prayer.

I have dozens of journals in which I poured out
my heart, wrote prayers, and sought the meaning of
the many vivid dreams God gave me on numerous
occasions. One day I was in great need of peace.
My husband at the time was on a business trip. Our
marriage had been struggling for years, so I cried
out to God to grant me another day without stress,
another day without having to face an argument or
the fear of having him home.

Later that night, my then-husband phoned to tell me he had missed his flight. He was shocked as that had never happened before in the hundreds of flights he had flown. For a reason he could not comprehend, everything went wrong and forced him to fly home the next day.

As I praised the LORD for giving me peace, I knew without a doubt He heard and answered my prayer. God, in His grace, had compassion on me and granted me my desire. He took my hurting heart and showed me clearly how very close He was and how much He loved me. I will never forget that night and the relief I felt knowing I could be at peace alone with God for one more day.

Do you believe that nothing is a miracle or that everything is a miracle? What experiences in your life caused you, or inspired you, to feel the way you do?

_____

_____

_____

_____

_____

_____

_____

_____

_____

Do you know someone who has, or have you yourself, witnessed a miracle? Describe what happened. How did it change you or the other person?

_____

_____

_____

_____

_____

_____

_____

_____

_____

What miracle do you need to happen in your life today? Write a letter to God asking Him to hear and answer your prayer, assuring Him you will not miss the miracle. Be sure to thank Him in advance for the way He will work behind the scenes to answer.

_____

_____

_____

_____

_____

_____

_____

**"Sing and make music from your heart
to the Lord, always giving thanks to God
the Father for everything, in the name
of our Lord Jesus Christ."
—Eph. 5:19b-20**

How many times has your family or friends said, "Please stop singing," or perhaps moved to another room or pressed earbuds in their ears to drown out your joyful noise? My daughter is one of those people who has listened to so much music all her life she knows the words to thousands of songs. If it's playing on the radio, she will likely be singing along, often much louder than the original artist. Thankfully, she has a pretty good voice, so it's not all that bad to listen to.

When it comes to "always giving thanks to God the Father for everything," that's a tougher sell. Everything? The economy is crushing us. We can hardly make ends meet. How do we thank God for that? Our children push back against everything we say. We feel disrespected and sometimes unloved, though we continue to care for them. The neighbors are messy and noisy, and on and on we go. How do find our way to thanksgiving in the midst of the world we live in?

I like to think that Paul was writing about giving thanks for the things that are not really "things." Even when our spouse is critical, we can be thankful we have a spouse. Many single people would be grateful to share their lives with someone and not be alone. If our children express disrespect, we need to discipline but can also be thankful God gave us children. Those who are unable to bear a child would be grateful to have them in their lives. When we feel unappreciated and undervalued at work, we can be grateful we have a job and the income and benefits that go with it.

So much of the "giving thanks for everything" involves a mindset of gratitude. When we focus on what is good, our mental, spiritual, psychological, and physical bodies respond through lowered blood pressure, increased peace and joy in our hearts, and minds that rest as they trust God to work all things together for good. There is always something small to be grateful for. Sometimes it just takes a little more work to see it.

Name something you are struggling with today.

_____

_____

_____

_____

_____

If you could change one thing about that person or situation, what would it be?

_____

_____

_____

_____

_____

_____

_____

What small part of that struggle can you find to be thankful for? Are you learning something through the struggle? Is someone growing through the confusion, frustration, or pain?

_____

_____

_____

_____

_____

_____

_____

_____

_____

_____

_____

_____

Where do you see God in your situation? Have you told Him how grateful you are that He is with you and is working to bring something good from the struggle?

As God spoke the world into being with and through Jesus, the Word, there is power in the words we speak aloud in Jesus' Name. In Deuteronomy 30, Moses exhorted the Israelites to obey God so they would be greatly blessed. In verse 19, Moses said, "... I have set before you life and death, blessings and curses. Now **choose life**, so that you and your children may live and that you may love the LORD your God, listen to his voice, and hold fast to him. For the LORD is your life..."

Choose life today and write God a note of gratitude or speak your grateful words aloud that you too will be greatly blessed.

_____

_____

_____

_____

_____

_____

_____

_____

_____

_____

**"Gratitude is a spiritual currency that
we can mint for ourselves and spend
without fear of bankruptcy."
—Fred Dewitt VanAmburgh**

I have been diving into the study of Spiritual Currency the past six months or so, and it makes so much sense. Spiritual Currency is considered to include love, compassion, gratitude, wisdom, and self-awareness – all important attributes for us to develop and share with the world. All attributes we can "mint" like currency or develop within ourselves as we press into God, Jesus Christ, and the Holy Spirit within us.

We carry the heart of Christ inside us, the Spirit of God in our own spirits. Jesus said we would "do greater things" than He did on earth. I wonder if part of the "greater thing" is developing the five attributes listed above—attributes that Jesus exhibited each day.

On that list, gratitude is placed firmly in the middle as a solid central theme. We know the power it has to change our lives and the lives of those around us. A couple of months ago, my husband came to me and made a negative comment about something going on at work. Before thinking about it, I stated, "I have a bubble of positivity and gratitude around me. Nothing negative is allowed to enter." I said it with great love for him, with no animosity or judgment. He just looked at me, stunned. Then he said, "Well, okay. It's not that big of a deal. I'll be fine." And off he went.

That's the power we carry inside us if we develop the gift of gratitude. We create a powerful, positive unseen force-field around us that is so strong that nothing negative can enter it. Isn't that what Jesus displayed in His personality and words? When he was criticized, he calmly replied. When the disciples argued around Him, He loved them and took time to teach them His ways. My desire is to grow to be as much like Jesus as I can, carrying His heart and spirit in me wherever I go, becoming a peacemaker in the world around me.

What are your thoughts about Spiritual Currency like gratitude? Who in your life most exhibits this gift – or any of the other categories of Spiritual Currency? Give examples.

_____

_____

_____

_____

_____

_____

_____

_____

_____

_____

_____

_____

_____

_____

_____

_____

_____

_____

_____

_____

What is one thing you could do to increase your thoughts of gratitude and positivity each day?

_____

_____

_____

_____

_____

_____

If you're a visual person, close your eyes and envision a bubble or shield of energy around you that negativity cannot penetrate. Within the bubble or shield is only the love and light of Christ. The bubble is not meant to repel others but is, instead, meant to radiate love, gratitude, and positivity. Can you feel it? Envision it? Describe what it means to you to know the positive power you have access to through developing spiritual currency in your heart through Holy Spirit and the love of God?

_____

_____

_____

_____

_____

_____

_____

_____

_____

_____

_____

_____

_____

_____

**"Let us come before him (the LORD)
with thanksgiving and glorify
(celebrate) him with music and song."
—Psalm 95:2**

As a former church worship singer, I love to glorify the LORD through music and song. It is not unusual for people to pass me on the road while I am praising God, mouth wide open, singing along with my Last Best Year Songs of Gratitude Spotify playlist at the top of my lungs. The windows are up, but I am confident God hears my voice and smiles. Our God loves a good celebration, particularly when worship is directed to Him.

I have not sung in public for 20-plus years, but recently my 96-year-old father-in-law who plays saxophone in a jazz band got me thinking that perhaps it would be fun to learn a couple of tunes to sing with the band. I jumped in with both feet, listened to countless jazz songs sung by females, selected two I liked best, and began to practice daily with a brand-new wireless microphone and mini-amp, compliments of Amazon Prime's one-day delivery.

Several months went by. I was feeling pretty good as I sang along with the female singers and the bands or orchestras that accompanied them. Then it got interesting. I asked my husband to listen to me and let me know if he thought I was ready to get on stage. Imagine my surprise when he said, "Can you sing it with a backtrack tape by yourself?" What? Without the actual singer? Just me? Um, probably not yet.

My father-in-law helped me find backtracks to practice with, but the sound just wasn't the same. My own voice was not nearly as wonderful to listen to when it was the only voice being heard. I liked it much better when I was singing with someone else. My re-imagined career as a singer is on hold, but I love to sing loud at church and join others around me as we worship the LORD with one voice. For now, that is more than enough for me.

Are you gifted with musical abilities to sing or play an instrument as unto the LORD? How have you used that gift in the past, and what are you doing today to glorify Him with your gift(s)?

_____

_____

_____

_____

_____

_____

_____

_____

_____

_____

_____

_____

_____

_____

_____

_____

_____

_____

If you're like me and you stopped singing or playing for a reason you can't even recall, are you sensing God reigniting that passion and gift? What has held you back from sharing your talent?

_____

_____

_____

_____

_____

_____

What can you do to work toward singing or playing again, or get involved in another way? What would that look like? Who do you need to talk with to take the first step? What is the current desire of your heart?

_____

_____

_____

_____

_____

_____

_____

_____

_____

_____

_____

_____

_____

_____

_____

_____

_____

_____

"Gratitude is an antidote to negative emotions, a neutralizer of envy, hostility, worry, and irritation."
—deavita

The audio book spoke loudly to my soul as I drove more than 450 miles to my destination. Life was full of worry, fear, and doubt – so much so that I contacted a therapist at our new church to discuss the situation with her. I was at a crossroad, envying others who seemed to float through life without marriage or career struggles. My heart was breaking, and I needed help to fix it.

At a long stoplight, I had a couple of minutes to peruse available audiobooks in my Audible app. Near the top of the list was *Change Your Paradigm, Change Your Life*. The title alone caught my attention as I wondered if a simple paradigm shift could really change my life. Three and a half hours later, I found myself feeling energized, positive, and hopeful. I was still thirty minutes away from the condo I was heading toward for a writer's retreat, so I re-started the book again and continued to listen over and over throughout the week.

Surprisingly, the truths and suggestions mentioned throughout the book did help me begin to change my paradigm. God has a purpose for each of our lives. It doesn't matter what anyone else is accomplishing. We have our own desires that we are intended to pursue. Why look to the left or the right when there is so much good in front of us? Today is a new day, and I am excited to live in this moment, grateful for today and for the joy of what is to come.

What about you? Who do you envy? What do they have or what have they accomplished that causes you to feel that way?

_____

_____

_____

_____

_____

_____

_____

_____

_____

In *Change Your Paradigm, Change Your Life*, the author states that we are capable of doing anything we have the *desire* to do. If we cannot do something, we likely don't have a desire to do it. How do you feel about that statement? Name one thing you believe you truly desire to accomplish or experience. How confident are you that God placed that desire inside you?

_____

_____

_____

_____

_____

_____

_____

_____

_____

What will it take for you to accomplish your desire?

_____

_____

_____

_____

_____

_____

_____

_____

In the book, I learned that it is critical you see yourself as already accomplishing the goal, that you view the goal from the end where you've already accomplished it. The paradigm shift then takes place in your mind, then your subconscious, and you begin to act in such a way as to bring that desire or goal to fruition. Visualize your accomplished desire in your mind, write it down, take a photo or clip a picture from a magazine that shows what you want. Look at it every day and say, "I am happy and grateful now that... (your accomplished goal)." (i.e. I am happy and grateful now that I am a successful business owner or I get to stay home with my children.)

_____

_____

_____

_____

_____

_____

_____

_____

_____

_____

"...sing psalms, hymns and spiritual songs with gratitude in your hearts to God.

And whatever you do, whether in word or deed, do it all in the name of the Lord Jesus, giving thanks to God the Father through him."
—Col. 3:16-17

Do it all in the name of Jesus, giving thanks to God through him? That sounds like a tall order to me, not that I don't want to do that very thing. I just know that in the normal course of the day, I sometimes get a little testy, especially if I am tired or hungry. Praise God I'm not one of those people who get literally "hangry." I've seen that, and it ain't pretty. Still, now that I know about changing my paradigm (attitude), I know I can do better, and I absolutely want to.

God illustrated this point so beautifully as I was driving to Hilton Head yesterday. I was already nearing the 9-hour drive point when a harsh rainstorm seemed to blow in from nowhere. Cars that had been traveling at 80 miles per hour were suddenly creeping along at 20 mph as the rain pelted windshields and tires splashed through puddles of water.

My first instinct was to be angry because I was tired and hungry. After stating my intense displeasure aloud to God, it struck me that it was a perfect time to say, "I am happy and thankful that I am safely in the condo on Hilton Head Island enjoying a restful night." And so, I did. I even said it twice for good measure.

Do you want to know what happened? The rain did not immediately cease, but no more than a few minutes later it was a trickle. Then the sun came out! Perhaps gratitude and confident praise to God is more powerful than we know. Some could say that was a coincidence, but I believe that God blessed me in that moment by calming the storm so I could get safely where I wanted to go.

What do you think? Have you ever actively practiced speaking gratitude over your life? If so, how did it make you feel? What happened as a result of that statement of gratitude?

_____

_____

_____

_____

_____

_____

_____

_____

_____

_____

_____

_____

_____

_____

_____

_____

_____

Describe a desire you'd like to express gratitude for today, whether in anticipation of something changing or gratitude for a desire or goal you have. What resources will you need to accomplish your desire or goal?

Affirm your confidence in God and trust Him to bring people and resources to you to help fulfill your desire or accomplish your goal in His time.

_____

_____

_____

_____

_____

_____

This is no secret at all. Gratitude is said to open the gates of heaven. God loves to hear our thanksgiving. Do you believe God's desire is to help you fulfill *your* desire? Speaking gratitude in advance of fulfilling a desire helps to change our attitude to one that is more confident and hopeful. This, in turn, causes us to *act* more confident and hopeful, which leads to success. Are you ready to give it a try? If yes, describe how this process makes you feel. If no, explain why.

_____

_____

_____

_____

_____

_____

_____

_____

_____

_____

_____

_____

_____

_____

"Gratitude is the fairest blossom which springs from the soul."
—Henry Ward Beecher

I am no gardener, but I do appreciate beautiful flowers in bloom and resonate with blossoms that spring forth from the ground in early March announcing the beginning of a new thing. Thanks to God's amazing plan, new life is being birthed and we get to appreciate its beauty as it grows. It is a stunning sight to behold.

In the same way, when we are open to receiving Divine energy through Holy Spirit, the seeds of good ideas come to us. Our job is to stay focused on the things our soul desires to experience in this lifetime. We are the creator of our own reality. It's taken me months to grasp that truth. My life today is a product of my past choices and decisions.

Sometimes things happen to us; but for the most part, we are the creators of the lives we live. Our thoughts become words, and our words become actions. There is such power in recognizing that. If we aim our attention solely on things that spark deep joy from within, our passion coupled with an attitude of gratitude and a determined plan of action, will lead us toward our desired goals.

Our job is to move forward regardless of mistakes. That is how we learn. It is how our soul grows. Keep moving, continue to take action. Whatever we give our time and energy to will grow so create a life you truly desire rather than focus on what does not inspire.

How does this day's message make you feel?

Do you agree that you are the creator of your own life, or in its purest form, *co-creator* with God? Explain why or why not.

_____

_____

_____

_____

_____

_____

_____

_____

_____

_____

_____

_____

_____

What are you giving your time and energy to now that you are most passionate about? How do you feel when you are pursuing that desire or goal?

_____

_____

_____

_____

_____

_____

_____

_____

What are you doing that does not inspire you? What percentage of time and energy are you giving to it? How do you feel when you are giving your energy to it? What can you do to reduce the time you give to it?

_____

_____

_____

_____

_____

_____

_____

Which decisions and choices in your past do you recognize as being part of your life creation? Which decisions and choices led you toward your desires and dreams, and which ones led you further away?

_____

_____

_____

_____

_____

_____

_____

_____

_____

_____

_____

_____

_____

_____

_____

_____

_____

_____

What do you want to change about your current way of life? What do you really want? Be as specific as possible listing every area from relationships to family to career to interests you are passionate about to desires and dreams and goals. Leave nothing out. The entire page following this is left blank for you to include as much as you want.

_____

_____

_____

_____

_____

_____

_____

_____

_____

_____

_____

_____

_____

_____

_____

_____

_____

_____

**"Give thanks to the LORD, call on his name; make known among the nations what he has done."
—1 Chr. 16:8**

The first verse of what is considered in the Bible as *David's Psalm of Thanks* is a beautiful summary of David's heart toward God and all He had done for him. David had recently been anointed king over Israel, had defeated the Philistines not once, but twice, as they attempted to overtake the new king and his kingdom. David was ecstatic, to say the least. He inquired of God before he went to battle and, both times, God was faithful to direct his steps and lead him and his army to victory.

David was a dreamer, but God spoke clearly to David's spirit so David knew the dreams he dreamed and the goals he set were God-ordained and, therefore, certain to come true. What does this mean for us? It means we study David's ways with God and mimick his unbridled love of God, always seeking God's wisdom before taking a step.

I can be very extroverted around people I know and love, but mostly I am more introverted and not usually one to share a lot about myself or God's work in and through me. 'You're no better than anyone else' my mother would say, though I never really thought I was. I just wanted to live a life of adventure and reach for goals and dreams that others might not want badly enough to persevere, accomplish, and see their dreams come true. I was a dreamer then and still am.

Today, however, I am learning how to be more like David, to pray and listen for God's direction before taking action. I am great at praying. It's the patient listening and trusting that God will answer that I'm working on. What I pray is that when I am reunited with Creator God in heaven one day and my journals are being read by those I leave behind, they will see an increasing desire to hear from God and follow in His way. When I am patient, God is always faithful to lead me. It's all in my journals. Maybe this guided journal will become one of those legacy items for you too.

Write about a circumstance in your life that requires you to make a decision or take action. How long have you been deliberating about what to do and when? Have you asked God what He wants you to do? If yes, what did you hear Him say?

_____

_____

_____

_____

_____

_____

_____

_____

_____

_____

_____

_____

_____

_____

_____

_____

_____

_____

_____

_____

_____

David was truly a man after God's own heart who was not afraid to dance and worship the LORD with his whole being. He was bold in proclaiming what the LORD had done for him. On a scale of 1 (lowest) to 10 (highest), how bold are you in proclaiming the good things the LORD has done for you?

_____

_____

_____

_____

_____

_____

_____

_____

_____

_____

List some ways to share God's goodness and answered prayers that are comfortable for you? Be sure to include face to face, social media, blog, newsletter, church bulletin, email, text, and any other ways you can think of. Then name one way to share what God has done for you that would take you outside of your comfort zone.

_____

_____

_____

_____

_____

_____

_____

_____

_____

_____

_____

_____

_____

_____

_____

_____

_____

_____

_____

_____

Make a commitment today to lean into the brave thing to proclaim the goodness of God in a new and exciting way. You just might discover a new gift inside that has been patiently waiting to make itself known to you and the world.

> **"Today be thankful and think
> how rich you are.
> Your family is priceless.
> Your health is wealth.
> Your time is gold."**
> **—Zig Ziglar**

There has never been a time in recent history that this quote has rung truer. Having endured and survived the COVID pandemic, the near collapse of our economy, and the continuing exposure and arrest of people who deceived our nation for many years, we need solid reasons to be grateful. Prices are too high, and people are suffering. What do we have to be grateful for?

Zig Ziglar was known for his infectious positivity, and the truth is, he was right. Our families *are* priceless. Our health *is* true wealth. What can we do without it? And our time, which we can never seem to get enough of, is pure gold. What would the world look like if we all focused on those three things, along with faith, hope, and love? I have to believe it would be heaven on earth.

My daughter called today. She and my grandson live 2,000 miles away, and she is missing being near family. They moved three years ago, so you would think it gets easier, but when holidays come and go and there's no family near to celebrate with, she and my grandson feel a little low. Family is everything. That's why I try to make regular trips to Colorado to see them, because I miss them too.

Last year, my husband and I were there helping to move a marble-top dining room table. As I huffed and puffed and lifted, something in my back popped. I felt okay for a bit, but later that night, I was down for the count. Months later, after working with a chiropractor on a weekly basis, my back finally felt better. It's still weaker than it used to be, but being so limited in mobility while I was injured taught me the value of having good health. It was no fun for me or for anyone around me.

As for time, our society has gotten so used to being busy that we don't even seem to realize how we are spending our days, weeks, and months running from place to place, often without much connection, meaning, or productivity. We scroll through social media, play games on our phones, watch videos, text, email, even watch movies, but at the end of the day, I'm not sure we can point to much that we saw or heard that meant anything. It was, for the most part, entertainment, which isn't all bad, but anything done to the extreme tends to be unhealthy.

I think maybe that's why Zig Ziglar said time is gold. Because it's a precious commodity that we can easily take for granted and we have a hard time investing and holding onto it. The old saying, "Buy land. They're not making anymore of it," holds true for time. We should want to use it wisely and preserve it as we rest and connect and enjoy as much of it as we can because we will never get back the hours, weeks, months, and years we already spent.

What is your favorite way to spend your time? Write your typical weekday schedule below noting the amount of time you spend doing each activity. Then do the same for the weekend.

_____

_____

_____

_____

_____

_____

_____

_____

_____

_____

_____

_____

_____

_____

_____

What do you notice about the way you spend your time? What consumes most of your time outside of work? Family? Entertainment? Social Media? Exercise? Reading, or another activity? Total the hours spent in an average week doing each activity.

_____

_____

_____

_____

_____

_____

_____

_____

Which activities bring you life, energy, and joy?

_____

_____

_____

_____

_____

_____

_____

_____

What specifically drains your energy when you participate in those activities? Which activities would you like to reduce or eliminate from your weekly schedule?

_____

_____

_____

_____

_____

_____

_____

_____

What is one step you could take to reduce or eliminate one of those activities today?

_____

_____

_____

_____

_____

_____

_____

_____

Who will you share your plan with? Who will hold you accountable and support you?

_____

_____

_____

_____

_____

_____

_____

_____

On a scale of 1(lowest) to 10 (highest), how committed are you to taking this step and moving toward a more energetic, productive, joy-filled life? When will you begin?

_____

_____

_____

_____

_____

_____

_____

_____

"But thanks be to God! He gives us the victory through our Lord Jesus Christ."
—1 Cor. 15:57

And so, we arrive at the end of this Guided Gratitude Journal and conclude with an excellent verse that reminds us of what we are most grateful for. No matter how the world sees us or treats us, our ultimate victory is in being reunited with Christ, the Father, and Holy Spirit. It only took me six decades to figure that out. Hopefully you are a faster learner than I am.

Despite writing for the Christian market, marketing efforts, and jockeying for positions to talk with agents and editors work pretty much the same as the world. I know because I have attended secular writer's conferences as well as Christian conferences. Some are very good at placing God first and avoiding much of the competition and drama, but most operate in a similar manner causing attendees to feel like they need to battle for position instead of trusting God to connect them with the right people.

Business is business and the bottom line is, can they make enough money to stay in business? I get it. I really do. It's just a difficult scenario to contend with if your heart is truly sold out to Jesus. Maybe you can relate.

Are you competing at work for a promotion or raise? Is there a small group of people at your child's school that seem to care more about their own desires than what's best for the students or staff? Are you a single mother who is being rejected by moms who have husbands at home because they don't understand you or fear you have designs on their husbands and are seeking to take their place?

Competition is everywhere, and Satan does some of his best (or should I say worst) work in the midst of it. He brings fear, doubt, confusion, envy, jealousy, and greed. He causes us to believe we need to defeat someone else in order to get what we desire or deserve. But he is a liar and a thief, a stealer of joy and a destroyer of love and trust.

And because we know that, our task is to focus on our eternal victory while we listen to God for His wisdom and guidance. As long as we are counting on God to fill us and lead us, we get to rest, relax, and run a victory lap.

In what area have you been the most competitive? How does it make you feel? Why was it so important to you?

_____

_____

_____

_____

_____

_____

_____

_____

_____

When have you trusted God to "work all things for good" and relaxed enough to allow his will to be done? What were you feeling then?

_____

_____

_____

_____

_____

_____

_____

_____

Name one situation you will give to God as you allow peace to fill your heart and mind. Who will you turn to for support to remind you of your decision?

_____

_____

_____

_____

"In ordinary life we hardly realize that we receive a great deal more than we give, and that it is only with gratitude that life becomes rich."

—Dietrich Bonhoeffer, Theologian

DAILY GRATITUDE PAGES

There is always something to be thankful for. Whether in your family, career, spiritual life, relationships with others, nature, purpose and meaning, learning/education, or desires of your heart, acknowledging the little things and thanking God 5 minutes each day, 7 days a week, for 7 weeks will cause it to become a habit and will lead to a more positive life.

It is a scientific fact. Give it a try! What have you got to lose?

Date: _____

Today I am grateful for...

1. _____

_____

2. _____

_____

3. _____

_____

4. _____

_____

5. _____

_____

6. _____

_____

7. _____

_____

8. _____

_____

9. _____

_____

10. _____

_____

Date: _____

Today I am grateful for...

1. _____

_____

2. _____

_____

3. _____

_____

4. _____

_____

5. _____

_____

6. _____

_____

7. _____

_____

8. _____

_____

9. _____

_____

10. _____

_____

Date: _____

Today I am grateful for...

1. _____

_____

2. _____

_____

3. _____

_____

4. _____

_____

5. _____

_____

6. _____

_____

7. _____

_____

8. _____

_____

9. _____

_____

10. _____

_____

Date: _____

Today I am grateful for...

1. _____

    _____

2. _____

    _____

3. _____

    _____

4. _____

    _____

5. _____

    _____

6. _____

    _____

7. _____

    _____

8. _____

    _____

9. _____

    _____

10. _____

     _____

Date: _____

Today I am grateful for...

1. _____

_____

2. _____

_____

3. _____

_____

4. _____

_____

5. _____

_____

6. _____

_____

7. _____

_____

8. _____

_____

9. _____

_____

10. _____

_____

Date: _____

Today I am grateful for...

1. _____

   _____

2. _____

   _____

3. _____

   _____

4. _____

   _____

5. _____

   _____

6. _____

   _____

7. _____

   _____

8. _____

   _____

9. _____

   _____

10. _____

    _____

Date: _____

Today I am grateful for...

1. _____

   _____

2. _____

   _____

3. _____

   _____

4. _____

   _____

5. _____

   _____

6. _____

   _____

7. _____

   _____

8. _____

   _____

9. _____

   _____

10. _____

    _____

Date: _____

Today I am grateful for...

1. _____

_____

2. _____

_____

3. _____

_____

4. _____

_____

5. _____

_____

6. _____

_____

7. _____

_____

8. _____

_____

9. _____

_____

10. _____

_____

Date: _____

Today I am grateful for...

1. _____

   _____

2. _____

   _____

3. _____

   _____

4. _____

   _____

5. _____

   _____

6. _____

   _____

7. _____

   _____

8. _____

   _____

9. _____

   _____

10. _____

    _____

Date: _____

Today I am grateful for...

1. _____

_____

2. _____

_____

3. _____

_____

4. _____

_____

5. _____

_____

6. _____

_____

7. _____

_____

8. _____

_____

9. _____

_____

10. _____

_____

Date: _____

Today I am grateful for...

1. _____

   _____

2. _____

   _____

3. _____

   _____

4. _____

   _____

5. _____

   _____

6. _____

   _____

7. _____

   _____

8. _____

   _____

9. _____

   _____

10. _____

    _____

Date: _____

Today I am grateful for...

1. _____

_____

2. _____

_____

3. _____

_____

4. _____

_____

5. _____

_____

6. _____

_____

7. _____

_____

8. _____

_____

9. _____

_____

10. _____

_____

Date: _____

Today I am grateful for...

1. _____

_____

2. _____

_____

3. _____

_____

4. _____

_____

5. _____

_____

6. _____

_____

7. _____

_____

8. _____

_____

9. _____

_____

10. _____

_____

Date: _____

Today I am grateful for...

1. _____

_____

2. _____

_____

3. _____

_____

4. _____

_____

5. _____

_____

6. _____

_____

7. _____

_____

8. _____

_____

9. _____

_____

10. _____

_____

Date: _____

Today I am grateful for...

1. _____

_____

2. _____

_____

3. _____

_____

4. _____

_____

5. _____

_____

6. _____

_____

7. _____

_____

8. _____

_____

9. _____

_____

10. _____

_____

Date: _____

Today I am grateful for...

1. _____
   _____

2. _____
   _____

3. _____
   _____

4. _____
   _____

5. _____
   _____

6. _____
   _____

7. _____
   _____

8. _____
   _____

9. _____
   _____

10. _____
    _____

Date: _____

Today I am grateful for...

1. _____

_____

2. _____

_____

3. _____

_____

4. _____

_____

5. _____

_____

6. _____

_____

7. _____

_____

8. _____

_____

9. _____

_____

10. _____

_____

Date: _____

Today I am grateful for...

1. _____
   _____

2. _____
   _____

3. _____
   _____

4. _____
   _____

5. _____
   _____

6. _____
   _____

7. _____
   _____

8. _____
   _____

9. _____
   _____

10. _____
   _____

Date: _____

Today I am grateful for...

1. _____

_____

2. _____

_____

3. _____

_____

4. _____

_____

5. _____

_____

6. _____

_____

7. _____

_____

8. _____

_____

9. _____

_____

10. _____

_____

Date: _____

Today I am grateful for...

1. _____

   _____

2. _____

   _____

3. _____

   _____

4. _____

   _____

5. _____

   _____

6. _____

   _____

7. _____

   _____

8. _____

   _____

9. _____

   _____

10. _____

    _____

Date: _____

Today I am grateful for...

1. _____

_____

2. _____

_____

3. _____

_____

4. _____

_____

5. _____

_____

6. _____

_____

7. _____

_____

8. _____

_____

9. _____

_____

10. _____

_____

Date: _____

Today I am grateful for...

1. _____
   _____

2. _____
   _____

3. _____
   _____

4. _____
   _____

5. _____
   _____

6. _____
   _____

7. _____
   _____

8. _____
   _____

9. _____
   _____

10. _____
    _____

Date: _____

Today I am grateful for...

1. _____

   _____

2. _____

   _____

3. _____

   _____

4. _____

   _____

5. _____

   _____

6. _____

   _____

7. _____

   _____

8. _____

   _____

9. _____

   _____

10. _____

   _____

Date: _____

Today I am grateful for...

1. _____

   _____

2. _____

   _____

3. _____

   _____

4. _____

   _____

5. _____

   _____

6. _____

   _____

7. _____

   _____

8. _____

   _____

9. _____

   _____

10. _____

   _____

Date: _____

Today I am grateful for...

1. _____

   _____

2. _____

   _____

3. _____

   _____

4. _____

   _____

5. _____

   _____

6. _____

   _____

7. _____

   _____

8. _____

   _____

9. _____

   _____

10. _____

    _____

Date: _____

Today I am grateful for...

1. _____

_____

2. _____

_____

3. _____

_____

4. _____

_____

5. _____

_____

6. _____

_____

7. _____

_____

8. _____

_____

9. _____

_____

10. _____

_____

Date: _____

Today I am grateful for...

1. _____
   _____

2. _____
   _____

3. _____
   _____

4. _____
   _____

5. _____
   _____

6. _____
   _____

7. _____
   _____

8. _____
   _____

9. _____
   _____

10. _____
    _____

Date: _____

Today I am grateful for...

1. _____
   _____

2. _____
   _____

3. _____
   _____

4. _____
   _____

5. _____
   _____

6. _____
   _____

7. _____
   _____

8. _____
   _____

9. _____
   _____

10. _____
    _____

Date: _____

Today I am grateful for...

1. _____

_____

2. _____

_____

3. _____

_____

4. _____

_____

5. _____

_____

6. _____

_____

7. _____

_____

8. _____

_____

9. _____

_____

10. _____

_____

Date: _____

Today I am grateful for...

1. _____

_____

2. _____

_____

3. _____

_____

4. _____

_____

5. _____

_____

6. _____

_____

7. _____

_____

8. _____

_____

9. _____

_____

10. _____

_____

Date: _____

Today I am grateful for...

1. _____

   _____

2. _____

   _____

3. _____

   _____

4. _____

   _____

5. _____

   _____

6. _____

   _____

7. _____

   _____

8. _____

   _____

9. _____

   _____

10. _____

    _____

Date: _____

Today I am grateful for...

1. _____

   _____

2. _____

   _____

3. _____

   _____

4. _____

   _____

5. _____

   _____

6. _____

   _____

7. _____

   _____

8. _____

   _____

9. _____

   _____

10. _____

   _____

Date: _____

Today I am grateful for...

1. _____

_____

2. _____

_____

3. _____

_____

4. _____

_____

5. _____

_____

6. _____

_____

7. _____

_____

8. _____

_____

9. _____

_____

10. _____

_____

Date: _____

Today I am grateful for...

1. _____

_____

2. _____

_____

3. _____

_____

4. _____

_____

5. _____

_____

6. _____

_____

7. _____

_____

8. _____

_____

9. _____

_____

10. _____

_____

Date: _____

Today I am grateful for...

1. _____

   _____

2. _____

   _____

3. _____

   _____

4. _____

   _____

5. _____

   _____

6. _____

   _____

7. _____

   _____

8. _____

   _____

9. _____

   _____

10. _____

   _____

Date: _____

Today I am grateful for...

1. _____

_____

2. _____

_____

3. _____

_____

4. _____

_____

5. _____

_____

6. _____

_____

7. _____

_____

8. _____

_____

9. _____

_____

10. _____

_____

Date: _____

Today I am grateful for...

1. _____
   _____

2. _____
   _____

3. _____
   _____

4. _____
   _____

5. _____
   _____

6. _____
   _____

7. _____
   _____

8. _____
   _____

9. _____
   _____

10. _____
    _____

Date: _____

Today I am grateful for...

1. _____

    _____

2. _____

    _____

3. _____

    _____

4. _____

    _____

5. _____

    _____

6. _____

    _____

7. _____

    _____

8. _____

    _____

9. _____

    _____

10. _____

    _____

Date: _____

Today I am grateful for...

1. _____

   _____

2. _____

   _____

3. _____

   _____

4. _____

   _____

5. _____

   _____

6. _____

   _____

7. _____

   _____

8. _____

   _____

9. _____

   _____

10. _____

   _____

Date: _____

Today I am grateful for...

1. _____

_____

2. _____

_____

3. _____

_____

4. _____

_____

5. _____

_____

6. _____

_____

7. _____

_____

8. _____

_____

9. _____

_____

10. _____

_____

Date: _____

Today I am grateful for...

1. _____
   _____

2. _____
   _____

3. _____
   _____

4. _____
   _____

5. _____
   _____

6. _____
   _____

7. _____
   _____

8. _____
   _____

9. _____
   _____

10. _____
    _____

Date: _____

Today I am grateful for...

1. _____

_____

2. _____

_____

3. _____

_____

4. _____

_____

5. _____

_____

6. _____

_____

7. _____

_____

8. _____

_____

9. _____

_____

10. _____

_____

Date: _____

Today I am grateful for...

1. _____

_____

2. _____

_____

3. _____

_____

4. _____

_____

5. _____

_____

6. _____

_____

7. _____

_____

8. _____

_____

9. _____

_____

10. _____

_____

Date: _____

Today I am grateful for...

1. _____

   _____

2. _____

   _____

3. _____

   _____

4. _____

   _____

5. _____

   _____

6. _____

   _____

7. _____

   _____

8. _____

   _____

9. _____

   _____

10. _____

    _____

Date: _____

Today I am grateful for...

1. _____

    _____

2. _____

    _____

3. _____

    _____

4. _____

    _____

5. _____

    _____

6. _____

    _____

7. _____

    _____

8. _____

    _____

9. _____

    _____

10. _____

    _____

Date: _____

Today I am grateful for...

1. _____

_____

2. _____

_____

3. _____

_____

4. _____

_____

5. _____

_____

6. _____

_____

7. _____

_____

8. _____

_____

9. _____

_____

10. _____

_____

Date: _____

Today I am grateful for...

1. _____

_____

2. _____

_____

3. _____

_____

4. _____

_____

5. _____

_____

6. _____

_____

7. _____

_____

8. _____

_____

9. _____

_____

10. _____

_____

Date: _____

Today I am grateful for...

1. _____

_____

2. _____

_____

3. _____

_____

4. _____

_____

5. _____

_____

6. _____

_____

7. _____

_____

8. _____

_____

9. _____

_____

10. _____

_____

Date: _____

Today I am grateful for...

1. _____

_____

2. _____

_____

3. _____

_____

4. _____

_____

5. _____

_____

6. _____

_____

7. _____

_____

8. _____

_____

9. _____

_____

10. _____

_____

Date: _____

Today I am grateful for...

1. _____

_____

2. _____

_____

3. _____

_____

4. _____

_____

5. _____

_____

6. _____

_____

7. _____

_____

8. _____

_____

9. _____

_____

10. _____

_____

Date: _____

Today I am grateful for...

1. _____

_____

2. _____

_____

3. _____

_____

4. _____

_____

5. _____

_____

6. _____

_____

7. _____

_____

8. _____

_____

9. _____

_____

10. _____

_____

Date: _____

Today I am grateful for...

1. _____

_____

2. _____

_____

3. _____

_____

4. _____

_____

5. _____

_____

6. _____

_____

7. _____

_____

8. _____

_____

9. _____

_____

10. _____

_____

Date: _____

Today I am grateful for...

1. _____

   _____

2. _____

   _____

3. _____

   _____

4. _____

   _____

5. _____

   _____

6. _____

   _____

7. _____

   _____

8. _____

   _____

9. _____

   _____

10. _____

    _____

Date: _____

Today I am grateful for...

1. _____

_____

2. _____

_____

3. _____

_____

4. _____

_____

5. _____

_____

6. _____

_____

7. _____

_____

8. _____

_____

9. _____

_____

10. _____

_____

Date: _____

Today I am grateful for...

1. _____

_____

2. _____

_____

3. _____

_____

4. _____

_____

5. _____

_____

6. _____

_____

7. _____

_____

8. _____

_____

9. _____

_____

10. _____

_____

Date: _____

Today I am grateful for...

1. _____
   _____

2. _____
   _____

3. _____
   _____

4. _____
   _____

5. _____
   _____

6. _____
   _____

7. _____
   _____

8. _____
   _____

9. _____
   _____

10. _____
    _____

ACKNOWLEDGMENTS

My greatest appreciation for A Guided Gratitude Journal goes to God for inspiring me each day to write blogs, record podcasts, and create books and journals to encourage and inspire readers toward greater clarity and purpose.

I am also grateful to Janice LaVore-Fletcher, Founder and President of Christian Coach Institute, for training me to be an empathetic listener and powerful question asker. Her coach training is invaluable to me as I coach beginning writers toward their own dreams of book writing and publishing. It is my honor and pleasure to help each one fulfill their inspired calling and goal.

As a result of much counseling, healing, and growth, my daughter Lauren Skinner and I have learned to find the blessing in the broken and healing in the midst of hurtful situations. No matter the circumstances, Lauren has taught me how to stand firm and be strong in the face of adversity. Together, we have learned to seek reasons to be grateful because they are always there. I am exceptionally grateful God gave Lauren and my grandson, Bentley, to me. They challenge and teach me every day what it looks like to rely on God for miraculous answers to big prayers.

I pray that today will be a new beginning for you as you are encouraged by each word and thoughtful question contained in this journal. May God give you faith to believe and eyes to see His blessings so you will be filled to overflowing with gratitude, peace, and joy today and every day.

ABOUT THE AUTHOR

Donna Wyland is an award-winning author of fiction, nonfiction, and picture books. Her most recent gift book, *Last Best Year – A Short Guide to a Grateful Life* – is a Golden Scroll Award Winner, and her picture books, *'Twas the Night Before Jesus* and *Psalms in Rhyme for Little Hearts* were both Readers' Choice Award Finalists. *'Twas the Night Before Jesus* also won the Illumination Award Silver Medal and *Psalms in Rhyme for Little Hearts* was the Christian Indie Award winner for picture books.

Though she began a career in financial planning, God interrupted those plans and called her to write more than twenty years ago. Donna responded, "Yes, Lord," and today has numerous books, essays, and blogs attributed to her name.

In the future, Donna hopes to continue writing guided journals to encourage and inspire people's faith and confidence in God and themselves. As a Certified Christian Life Coach, Donna learned the value of asking powerful questions. Through her guided journals she hopes to lead readers to greater clarity, peace, and purpose as they read, consider, and reply to the questions asked.

Donna is grateful for her husband, four grown daughters, sons-in-law, and grandchildren. She and her husband currently live in Southwest Florida, but her passion for travel frequently takes her to other states and countries around the world. Only God knows where she will live in five years. Thankfully she has a husband who says he will follow her wherever she goes.

DONNA'S OTHER BOOKS

CHILDREN'S BOOKS

Psalms in Rhyme for Little Hearts
'Twas the Night Before Jesus
If I Could Ask Jesus
If I Could Ask Jesus Coloring Book
Your Home in Heaven
Your Home in Heaven Curriculum
Tu Casa en el Cielo (Spanish Edition)

ADULT BOOKS

Last Best Year—A Short Guide to a Grateful Life
Autum's Harmony
Surrender